D1283246

Teen Pregnancy

by Judy Berlfein

**LUCENT
B·O·O·K·S**

Look for these and other books in the Lucent Overview series:

Abortion
Acid Rain
AIDS
Alcoholism
Animal Rights
The Beginning of Writing
Cancer
Dealing with Death
Death Penalty
Drugs and Sports
Drug Trafficking
Eating Disorders

Endangered Species
Energy Alternatives
Extraterrestrial Life
Gangs
Garbage
Greenhouse Effect
Gun Control
Hazardous Waste
The Holocaust
Homeless Children
Ocean Pollution
Oil Spills

The Olympic Games
Ozone
Population
Rainforests
Recycling
Smoking
Special Effects in the
  Movies
Teen Alcoholism
Teen Pregnancy
The UFO Challenge
Vietnam

Library of Congress Cataloging-in-Publication Data

Berlfein, Judy, 1958-
　　Teen Pregnancy / by Judy Berlfein.
　　　　p.　cm. — (Lucent overview series)
　　Includes bibliographical references (p.90-91) and index.
　　Summary: Examines the prevalence and causes of teen pregnancy in the United
States and presents consequences and solutions.
　　ISBN 1-56006-130-8
　　1. Teenage parents—United States—Juvenile literature.
　2. Teenage pregnancy—United States—Juvenile literature.
　[1. Pregnancy.　2. Teenage parents.　3. Sex instruction for youth.]
　I. Title.　II. Series.
HQ759.64.B36　1992　　　　　　　　　　　　　　　　　　92-9673
362.83'92—dc20　　　　　　　　　　　　　　　　　　　　　　CIP
　　　　　　　　　　　　　　　　　　　　　　　　　　　　　　　AC

© Copyright 1992 by Lucent Books, Inc.
P.O. Box 289011, San Diego, CA 92198-9011

*To Dadla
for sharing with me the magical joys
and excruciating frustrations of parenting
and also
for endless patience as an editor*

Acknowledgments

The author wishes to thank all the individuals who contributed to this book through articles, books, or interviews, including:

Sharon Weremiuk, Antoinette Washington, and Alex Weir of the San Diego (California) Adolescent Pregnancy and Parenting Program (SANDAPP); Ruth Beaglehole of the Business Industry School, Los Angeles, California; and Carolyn Fryer of Life House, La Mesa, California.

Contents

1

It Can Happen
to Anyone

KATHERINE* WAS JUST finishing her last year of high school. Life seemed to be moving along smoothly. A promising future lay ahead as she eagerly awaited receiving her diploma.

"I never thought it would happen to me—that famous line," Katherine recounted. "When I discovered that I was pregnant, my boyfriend and I talked about it, but we never talked about an abortion. It was like a dream world, when you're little and you get your first baby doll—that's how I was thinking. But then you think, when you've got that baby doll, you could always throw it away when you're tired of it. But when you have a baby, you can't."

Though still a high school student, Katherine was forced to think about motherhood. One million other American teenagers become pregnant each year and face this same situation. That translates into one in every ten girls under the age of twenty. In the United States, thirteen hundred girls under the age of twenty will become mothers today. Of those young women, eight hundred will not yet have completed high school. And one hun-

(Opposite page) Although some teenagers know little about themselves and their bodies, pregnancy sometimes prompts them to learn more.

Author's Note: The names of the teenagers in this book have been changed to protect their identities.

dred will not have even reached the ninth grade. Five hundred additional girls will have abortions. Twenty-six thirteen- and fourteen-year-olds will give birth to their first child. Thirteen sixteen-year-olds will already be delivering their second child.

Changing attitudes

Teenage pregnancy is not a new phenomenon. In the past few decades, however, society's attitudes have changed significantly. And these changes have led to a new awareness of the problem.

In the 1950s, for example, pregnant girls were often sent away for nine months to stay with distant relatives or to live in homes for unwed mothers. Their children were frequently put up for adoption. Other parents strongly and sometimes forcefully encouraged marriage between the young parents. Until the early 1970s, pregnant teenagers were often not allowed to stay in school.

But times have slowly changed. When abortion became legal in 1973, many teenagers began choosing this option. And single parenting has gained more acceptance. In 1950, six out of seven pregnant girls married the father of the child. By 1987, those numbers had changed dramatically. Only one-third of the teenage couples expecting a baby chose marriage.

Tha Alan Guttmacher Institute, a research arm of the family planning organization Planned Parenthood, reports that 42 percent of teenage pregnancies in 1989 ended in abortion. Among those who gave birth, only 4 percent of the unmarried teenagers put their babies up for adoption.

The teenagers—still children themselves—who are conceiving their own children come from all walks of life. They live in urban ghettos, suburban neighborhoods, and rural communities.

Yet teenage pregnancy, studies show, is more

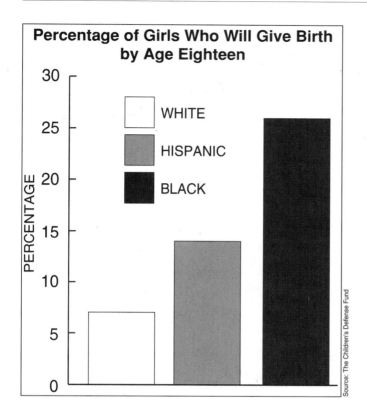

Percentage of Girls Who Will Give Birth by Age Eighteen

PERCENTAGE

WHITE
HISPANIC
BLACK

Source: The Children's Defense Fund

common among some groups than others. The Children's Defense Fund, a Washington, D.C.-based group working for the rights and protection of children, has found that early parenthood is most common among black teenagers. Their research has also shown that girls from disadvantaged homes are three to four times more likely to become mothers during their teenage years than those from middle- or upper-income homes.

Linnie, for example, grew up in one of the poorest sections of Washington, D.C. Two months before her twelfth birthday, she began having sex with her boyfriend, James, who was the same age. They did not use birth control, according to Linnie, because she was afraid of it. By the time Linnie reached fifteen, she was pregnant and James had left her and turned to crime.

An urban teenager and her child face many struggles of inner-city living.

Shortly before Linnie became pregnant, her mother died and her oldest brother was left to care for the family. Bad turned to worse when the family was thrown out of its apartment because of late rent payments. Linnie no longer had a home, and she was in her seventh month of pregnancy. During the next two years, she moved sixteen times—staying with her grandmother in Maryland, a boyfriend's aunt, and her brother's friends.

Linnie lived in an urban area where she faced one bad living situation after another. Pregnant teenagers in less populated areas of the nation also face obstacles.

A lack of prenatal care

In Mississippi and other rural areas, many teenagers give birth just as their mothers—who were also in their teens—had before them. The Williams sisters, Sheila and Charmaine, are one example. Their mother, Shavon Williams, had six children by the age of thirty-one. She delivered her first baby at fifteen. Her daughters gave birth within a few months of each other. Sheila was fourteen, and Charmaine had just celebrated her sixteenth birthday.

Pregnancy affects teenagers from all walks of life.

Unlike many teenage girls who become pregnant in rural America, the Williams sisters—who live in a small Mississippi town—saw a doctor during their pregnancies. Their mother drove them to a clinic several miles from home. Most of the other residents in the area do not have cars. So, many of the girls in the town do not see a doctor until they are on the delivery table.

Few girls from poor families make it to the doctor during pregnancy. Only 46 percent of all pregnant teenagers regularly visit a physician for prenatal care, which is care for the baby before it is born. In the end, the babies pay the price. According to the Children's Defense Fund, infants born to mothers who have not seen a doctor during pregnancy are forty times less likely to survive the first few months of life than babies born to mothers receiving adequate medical attention.

A pregnant fifteen-year-old discusses prenatal care. Fewer than half of all pregnant teenagers seek such care.

Some pregnant teenagers do make it to the doctor. But their concern is not for prenatal care. These teenagers are seeking abortions.

A mistaken assumption

Naomi is one of the many teenagers who chose abortion over giving birth. The decision to end the pregnancy was difficult, though for Naomi, the choice was clear. At nineteen, she did not feel prepared to raise a baby. Naomi had her heart set on medical school. While she planned and hoped to one day marry her boyfriend, David, whom she had dated for four years, neither felt ready to take that step yet.

Both attended college in a small town neighboring the Rocky Mountains. Both had always taken birth control very seriously. One afternoon, however, while making love, they believed Naomi was safe. Her period was due the next day, so they decided to not use birth control. They assumed she could not get pregnant so close to menstruation.

As a biology student, Naomi thought she understood the intricacies of her body's cycles. There are only a few days each month when the egg is available for fertilization by the sperm. Under most circumstances, this takes place approximately two weeks after menstruation. But the body is not always on schedule, and a woman's fertile period can change from month to month.

Although she thought it was impossible, Naomi became pregnant on that particular afternoon. Naomi knew immediately what she needed to do. She had an abortion. This was a painful decision, but the right one for her. Nevertheless, she told only one friend aside from her boyfriend about the experience. She felt too embarrassed and ashamed to discuss it with others. And even with David and her close friend, she had diffi-

Pregnant teenagers face many difficult decisions.

culty expressing the sadness that enveloped her. No one seemed to understand the turmoil she felt.

Although David did not experience the abortion firsthand, he did feel his own turmoil. He was there to hold Naomi's hand, to help pay the bill, and to join in the sadness.

Frequently, discussions of teenage pregnancy focus on girls because they bear the obvious results. The boy's role is often neglected. But pregnancy occurs because action is taken by males and females together. Neither role can be ignored.

While it is difficult to determine the exact figures, a National Center for Health Statistics report found that more than 100,000 teenage boys in the United States became fathers in 1987. What role did these young men play in raising their children?

Although many teenage fathers do not share in the responsibility of parenting, some find it a rewarding experience.

Teenage fathers

According to a 1989 article published by the Alan Guttmacher Institute, many fathers did not remain near their children for long. Eighty-four percent of the fathers lived away from the mother and child. Only one-third of the fathers continued to visit their children at least once a week after the children reached their first birthday.

While statistics show that many children of teenage mothers grow up without the influence of a father, some teenage fathers do try to take part in their child's life. Nathan is an example of a concerned father. At fourteen, he became sexually involved with his girlfriend, Janice. Growing up in a family of nine with little attention from his own father, Nathan knew he was not prepared for fatherhood. He insisted that Janice use birth control.

One year after they had begun dating, however, Janice told Nathan she was pregnant. He wanted to run and hide. He wanted to break all contact with her. He felt his life had been ruined.

His family, however, encouraged him to take part, to help out financially, and to become involved in raising his son. After his first visit with the infant, Nathan's anger melted and a determination grew inside of him. "He looked just like me, and I got to thinking that I was treating him the same way my dad had treated me. Somehow it just didn't seem fair," he said.

Nathan often felt isolated during those early years as a father. "It was hard for me, and sometimes I wanted to hide the fact that I was a father. I didn't want to tell people," he said. In spite of the loneliness, Nathan managed to work and complete college while still being a father.

A price to pay

Pregnant teenagers, young parents, and their children travel a difficult path. Babies suffer when their mothers receive inadequate prenatal care and take poor care of themselves. More than 10 percent of infants born to teenagers are addicted to drugs at birth, and many suffer from brain damage. Teenage mothers often drop out of

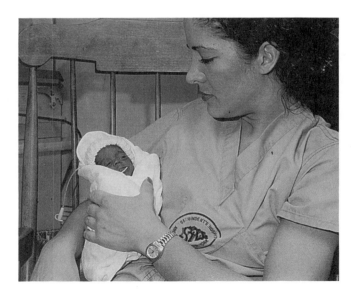

Teenagers who receive no prenatal care often give birth prematurely. A nurse holds a premature baby being fed through a tube.

Many teenage mothers drop out of school. Others, like this sixteen-year-old mother, finish high school and raise their children with the help of special programs.

school, and many must rely on public assistance to survive. They lose their chance for education, career opportunities, and the simple, carefree times of adolescence. Society pays a high price for supporting these young adults by providing tax money that buys their rent, food, child care, and health care.

Some pregnant teenagers do survive the turmoil and manage to finish their education, find a job, and raise their children to be useful members of society. But their path is littered with obstacles.

If teenage pregnancy has so many negative consequences, and creates so many problems, why do so many girls become pregnant? What motivates them to become mothers? That is a question posed frequently by researchers working in the field. Experts hope that by understanding these reasons, they can develop strategies to reduce the number of teenage pregnancies.

2

Why Are Teenagers Getting Pregnant?

GIRLS GET PREGNANT when they have sex and do not use birth control. Although approximately four million teenagers are sexually active in the United States, only half of them use any kind of protection. Those statistics help explain why one million teens become pregnant each year. But why are these young people having sex, and why are they not protecting themselves from the consequences?

The first question may be difficult to answer with a single response. For every potential explanation, there is a contradictory statement. Many people believe that sex education in the schools has made sex among teenagers more acceptable. Others argue that teenagers will have sex with or without sex education classes and that responsible decision making comes only with greater understanding and knowledge.

There are, however, many influences on a young person's life. One is the mass media. Each year, television displays twenty thousand scenes of suggested sexual intercourse. Ninety-four percent of the sexual encounters depicted on soap

(Opposite page) A barrage of myths and facts about sex confuses many teenagers. Friends, family, and the media often convey mixed messages.

Movies portray sex as exciting and romantic, but rarely depict the consequences of unprotected sex.

operas occur between unmarried couples. Teenagers are bombarded with images displaying the excitement and romance of sex each day on television and in the movies.

Mixed messages

Experts are not certain if portrayals of sex in the media cause teenagers to become sexually active or if these scenes merely reflect a society in which sex at an early age has become accepted. What is known, however, is that the media rarely present the consequences of unprotected sex, that is, having babies. During a passionate love scene, one almost never hears a man whisper sweetly to the woman, "Do you have any birth control?"

Many parents also shy away from teaching their children about responsible sexual behavior. In one 1988 survey, half of the teenagers interviewed said they would like to talk more with their parents about sex and that they would like their parents to provide more information.

Many parents and religious groups believe that sex before marriage is wrong, and they try to encourage teenagers to accept this view. But peer pressure and a culture that portrays sex as fun,

Experts debate whether portrayals of sex in the media cause teenagers to become sexually active, or merely reflect the reality that teenagers do engage in sex.

exciting, or even a way to prove one's maturity make abstinence difficult. Teenagers are left with conflicting messages.

Fifteen-year-old Susan summed up the dilemma. She is one of twenty teenage girls participating in a University of North Carolina media and sexuality study. In a journal she keeps for the study, Susan wrote: "One [song] really caught my attention. It was basically, 'Come over to my house so we can do it.' This represents sex as being O.K. Later I heard, 'Let's Wait a While,' by Janet Jackson. Which basically says, 'Let's not rush into it.' It's kind of hard as a teenager to decide what is right."

Birth control

Most young adults want to explore the unknown and act responsibly. Some people believe that if teenagers are going to be curious and experiment with sexual relations, they should take responsibility and protect themselves with birth control.

Birth control, or contraceptives, comes in several different forms. The most effective, reliable method of preventing pregnancy is abstinence, or not having sex at all. But even those who do engage in sexual activity can substantially decrease the odds of conceiving a child by using contraceptives.

Several methods are available through drugstores or physicians. Condoms, for example, are often the easiest option for boys. A condom is a rubber sheath that covers the penis and prevents sperm from entering the vagina. Condoms also offer protection against AIDS, a sexually transmitted disease. Girls have a wider range of choices: birth control pills, which must be taken daily; an intrauterine device (IUD), which is a plastic or metal device that the doctor inserts into the uterus; a diaphragm, a small rubber cup that is

In her song "Let's Wait a While" Janet Jackson urges young people to think before they act.

coated with a sperm-killing jelly and placed inside the vagina just before intercourse; a contraceptive sponge, which is similar to the diaphragm but is disposable; and a new device called Norplant. Norplant consists of six matchstick-size tubes that are inserted by a doctor beneath the skin under the arm. The tubes, which release hormones that prevent pregnancy, can be left in place for five years.

Often, teenagers are unaware of these birth control options. Even those who have learned about them from parents, school, or friends still may not know how to purchase contraceptives or may be unable to afford them. Others admit they are simply too lazy to protect themselves. They explain that sex just happens; it is not an anticipated event. Using birth control, however, requires planning. Teenagers frequently feel embarrassed, shy, or scared discussing sex in advance.

A young woman selects condoms from a drug store display.

"The first time, it was like totally out of the blue," sixteen-year-old Sarah from New York says. "You don't say, 'Well, I'm going to his house and he's probably going to try to go to bed with me, so I better make sure I'm prepared.' I mean you don't know it's coming, so how are you to be prepared?"

Some teenagers spurn birth control because they feel it makes it too easy to have sex too often. Eighteen-year-old Karen from Indiana finds it easier to occasionally risk having unprotected sex than to take responsibility for her actions. "If I did use a contraceptive," Karen says, "then I would have sex more. And I don't feel it's right. I haven't been raised that way. If I did use birth control, it would be too easy. Now, knowing there's a risk, it stops me."

Some teenagers forego birth control pills or other contraceptives because they do not know how to get them or are unwilling to take responsibility for their actions.

Misunderstandings

Young people often do not understand how their own bodies work. These misunderstandings can lead to pregnancy. Teenagers frequently comment: "I didn't think it could happen the first time." Contrary to this widely held belief, pregnancy can occur the first time or the fiftieth time. All that needs to take place is for the male's sperm to find and fertilize the female's egg. It does not make any difference how many times the couple has had intercourse.

What does matter is the egg. There must be an egg available for fertilizing. There are only a few days each month when the female is considered fertile. This is when the egg has been released from the ovary during ovulation and is in the appropriate location for joining with the sperm. Some people try to time intercourse to avoid these fertile periods and avoid pregnancy. This form of birth control is called the rhythm method. This method, however, is very risky. The time of

A NEW 27-MAN COMMITTEE REPORT TO SIR EDWARD BOYLE URGES FULLER SEX INSTRUCTION IN SCHOOLS

BIRDS AND BEES DEPARTMENT

INFORMATION

COMPLAINTS

FRANKLIN

month varies slightly from person to person. In addition, many teenagers have irregular menstrual cycles, which means that pinning down the exact fertile days can be close to impossible.

Sometimes, by chance, a girl does not get pregnant the first time or even the second or third. That simply means she has missed her fertile periods; it does not mean she cannot get pregnant. Every time she has intercourse, there is a chance she will get pregnant.

Some couples rely on what they believe to be a commonsense form of birth control. The male partner pulls his penis out before releasing the sperm. This can certainly decrease one's chances of pregnancy, but this method is much less reliable than using contraception. It is very easy for one tiny sperm out of the millions released to make its way up to the egg.

Many teenagers are confused by the barrage of myths and facts they receive from friends, family, and the media. And they often feel too embarrassed to talk openly about what they do not understand. Without talking openly, however, more confusion occurs. A boy may assume that the girl has taken care of birth control, while the girl may hope her partner knows what he is doing. And if nobody brings the subject up, a false assumption often leads to a pregnancy.

Discussing birth control

James is one of perhaps many teenage boys who are sexually active but are unwilling to discuss the issue of birth control. James is eighteen and lives in New York City. He views birth control as the girl's responsibility. If she does not take any precaution, it is up to her alone to deal with the consequences, he believes. It is difficult for him to realize that it takes two to make a baby and therefore both should be involved in prevention. "You can ask a girl if she is using contraceptives if you want to, but why do it?" he comments. "The girl is smart. I really don't think she would go through with it if she wasn't prepared. And I don't care if she is or not. That's her problem."

Sometimes, girls actually avoid discussing or using birth control because they are afraid of their partner's reaction. They are worried about appearing to be too cautious or too worried about unprotected sex. Or some girls are concerned that using birth control such as condoms may make sex less enjoyable for their partner. Negative reactions from boyfriends often reinforce these feelings. Eighteen-year-old Stacy from Chicago felt humiliated by her boyfriend's response to her request that he use a condom. "I felt guilty about using contraceptives because my boyfriend said,

Talking openly about birth control can help eliminate confusion and embarrassment.

'Oh, I don't want to put on this stupid wet suit.'"

Stacy was influenced by her boyfriend's reaction. She is not unusual. Many people, especially teenagers, care and worry about what friends think about them. Teenagers often like to take the accepted course, to do what everyone else is doing. If having sex without birth control is popular and accepted, then many will continue to do it.

Peer pressure

Junior high school counselor Veda Usilton worked at an inner-city school and saw the consequences of such peer pressure. After spending many hours talking with students, she summed up their feelings this way: "It's not cool to be an A student. It's not cool to be a virgin. It's not cool to say you're a virgin. You shouldn't be on birth control."

As a teenager, being cool is often of primary importance. Adolescence is a difficult time. Young people are defining their identities, trying to determine who they are. Peer pressure plays a major role. Teenagers will go to great lengths to fit into a group, hoping to appear mature and sophisticated and trying to gain respect. When their friends are having sex and not using birth control, many young people feel pressured to do the same.

"For many young men," says Alex Weir of San Diego Adolescent Pregnancy and Parenting Program, "peer pressure says, what makes them a man is how many babies they make. They are trying to prove their masculinity and their need to possess, to own, to be able to say this is mine; it's my son; it's my daughter. But they don't want the responsibility of taking care of it."

Aside from peer pressure, adolescents often seek a thrill from taking risks. Driving fast, experimenting with drugs, and engaging in sex without protection are often seen as adventures rather than dangers.

"Teenagers see themselves as immortal and invulnerable," says Bryan Robinson, author of a book about teenage fathers. "They do not realize that speeding may cause an accident, drugs can lead to addictions, and sex often ends in a baby."

Looking for love

Many teenagers feel distraught when they learn they are pregnant. But others have a completely different reaction. For them, news of a baby is a secret dream come true. Young adults living in poverty often feel their lives are going nowhere and that they have few chances for success. Having a baby represents one tangible accomplishment. "These kids feel that having a baby is one way they can achieve," author Robinson says. Others who come from homes filled with violence and despair often search for the love they never received. They hope to gain that love from an innocent child.

Sixteen-year-old Kendra from Illinois had a miscarriage during her first pregnancy. Her second baby died at birth. "I knew all about birth control," she says. "I wanted a child. I wanted something I could put my love into, something that could love me. I didn't know how else to do that. I feel if I'm to survive, I got to survive for someone else."

Kendra did not fight the strong feelings coming from within. She wanted a baby, got pregnant, and had one. Other teenagers realize that having a child brings not only rewards but also limits. A baby may offer love but it also disrupts education and career plans. Sometimes, however, the temptation for a child is too great to resist.

For Shawn, that was the case. She grew up in a poor urban neighborhood on the East Coast. All her friends were having babies at fifteen and six-

Some teenagers who are not loved by parents hope to gain love by having a child.

In some communities where education and job opportunities for teens are bleak, having a baby may represent a sign of accomplishment.

teen. Having a child was a sign of status and accomplishment among teenagers who had few other opportunities.

Filling a void

Shawn, on the other hand, understood the long-term drawbacks. When she looked at her friends who had babies, she saw how difficult their lives had become. She wanted a child but decided she would wait until she was older, employed, and married.

Slowly, the harsh conditions in which she lived eroded her resolve. Shawn's parents fought frequently, which created a tense atmosphere in her home. Her friends teased her because she was not having sex. All of this left her lonely and isolated. She felt distant from her bickering parents and alienated from her sexually active friends. As she fell deeper into depression, a baby seemed to be her only hope for salvation. Convinced that a child would renew her zest for life, Shawn became pregnant.

Many more girls like Shawn, and Kendra are having babies to fill a void in their lives. As one young teenager from a poor neighborhood told a reporter, "Girls know all about birth control. Girls out here get pregnant because they want to have babies. You need to learn what's going on inside people's homes these days!"

There are many reasons why teenagers engage in sex and ultimately become pregnant. It may be a lack of self-esteem or peer pressure. A girl may be trying to fill an emptiness in her life. A boy may be trying to prove his masculinity. Possibly, ignorance and simple laziness explain the situation. In all cases, however, the conscious or unconscious decision to become pregnant profoundly affects the course of both parents' lives. The teenage couple is forced to make a significant choice: abortion, adoption, or raise the child. Each choice leads down a different path to a different future.

3

Abortion and Adoption

SEVERAL DECADES AGO, most pregnant girls had few decisions to make. Usually, parents sent their daughters out of town for the necessary nine months. The girls would deliver in another city and promptly give the babies up for adoption. In other instances, an illegal abortion was discreetly arranged. Rarely would young girls keep the child to raise themselves. Times have changed. Today, pregnant teenagers are faced with a list of difficult choices. Girls can raise the child, alone or with the father; have an abortion; or give up the baby for adoption. When young adults choose parenthood, they decide to no longer lead the life of a carefree teenager.

Postponing parenthood

By giving the baby up for adoption or terminating the pregnancy with abortion, teenagers can eventually resume their old routines. Abortions and adoptions, however, rarely happen without emotional cost. While the outer world of these teenagers may appear unchanged, their inner life may be permanently altered.

Abortion and adoption are different options, but teens choose both paths for similar reasons—

(Opposite page) Today's pregnant teenagers have more choices than teenagers in the past. Ironically, more alternatives can make it even harder to make a decision.

Children require a great deal of attention and need food, clothing, and medical care. Teenagers who feel they cannot provide these things often choose abortion or adoption.

because they are not prepared to become parents. With parenting comes a long list of responsibilities that many adolescents are not ready to accept. Children need diapers, food, medical care, clothing, toys, and many other things. Most teenagers cannot afford such expenses. They can barely save money for their own needs.

Babies also demand lots of attention. The busy schedule of a junior high or high school student does not allow for sleepless nights with a crying child or long days with an active baby. Many teenagers realize they simply do not have the patience or have not achieved the maturity required for parenting. They are more interested in their own future and pursuing a career than in sharing their adolescence with a child.

Abortion on the rise

When these teenagers find themselves pregnant, they are faced with two choices: abortion or adoption. During the last few decades, abortion has become more common, while adoptions have decreased significantly. Neither choice is easy to make. Both actions can be emotionally painful and draining.

Once the least common response to teen preg-

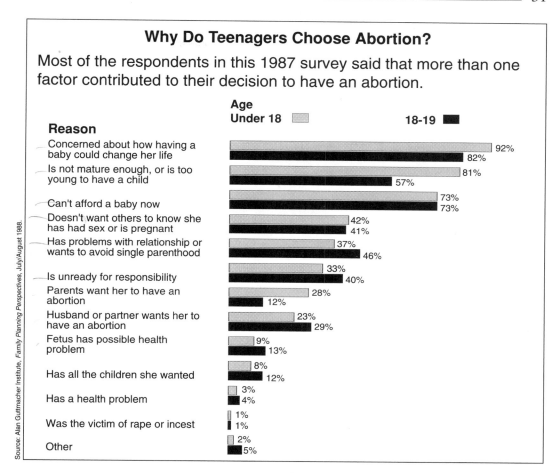

Why Do Teenagers Choose Abortion?

Most of the respondents in this 1987 survey said that more than one factor contributed to their decision to have an abortion.

Age
Under 18 □   18-19 ■

Reason

Reason	Under 18	18-19
Concerned about how having a baby could change her life	92%	82%
Is not mature enough, or is too young to have a child	81%	57%
Can't afford a baby now	73%	73%
Doesn't want others to know she has had sex or is pregnant	42%	41%
Has problems with relationship or wants to avoid single parenthood	37%	46%
Is unready for responsibility	33%	40%
Parents want her to have an abortion	28%	12%
Husband or partner wants her to have an abortion	23%	29%
Fetus has possible health problem	9%	13%
Has all the children she wanted	8%	12%
Has a health problem	3%	4%
Was the victim of rape or incest	1%	1%
Other	2%	5%

Source: Alan Guttmacher Institute, *Family Planning Perspectives*, July/August 1988.

nancy, abortion has gained considerable popularity since it became legal in the United States in 1973. Each year, 42 percent of pregnant teenagers obtain abortions.

The procedure itself may be simple, but reaching the decision to have an abortion can be agonizing. One of the first worries many pregnant girls have is confiding in their parents. Will they approve or disapprove? Should she tell them in the first place? Sometimes, a pregnant teenager does not have a choice. In at least thirty states, laws exist that require girls under eighteen to consult with their parents before having an abortion. This can have both positive and negative effects. Sometimes, a girl may be surprised to find how supportive her parents can be. Other parents may be less than understanding and may actually throw their daughter out of the house or physically abuse her for her actions.

In a tragic case, Becky sought an abortion at seventeen. In her home state of Indiana, she was required to gain permission from one parent. Rather than face her parents, she planned to go to Kentucky for the procedure. But Becky was nervous and did not want to wait the extra days. Instead, she tried to perform the abortion herself. She died in the attempt.

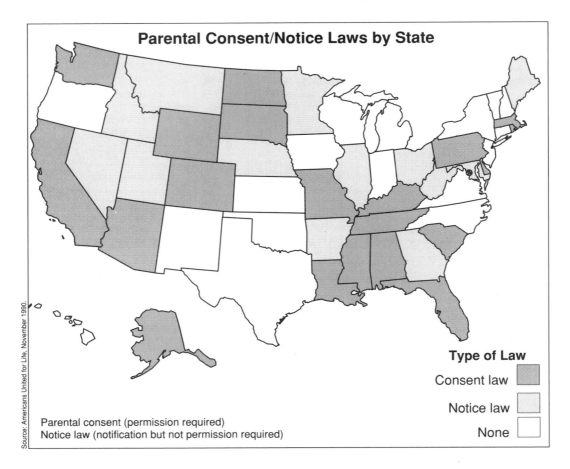

Parental Consent/Notice Laws by State

Source: Americans United for Life, November 1990.

Parental consent (permission required)
Notice law (notification but not permission required)

Type of Law

Consent law

Notice law

None

For some girls, parents can play a supportive role, helping their daughter decide the best route to take. Some people believe abortion is the least traumatic route, causing the fewest long-term disruptions in a young girl's life. Others believe abortion is morally wrong, that if a girl becomes pregnant, she is obligated to bring the child into the world, whether she takes on the parenting role or not. Teenagers may welcome their parents' input or reject it out of hand. In some instances, the parents themselves do not agree about what is best, and the daughter is caught in the middle.

Some pregnant girls fear talking to their parents about their situation, while others find their parents are helpful and supportive.

Family turmoil

Fourteen-year-old Denise who lived in Maryland found herself in this position, torn between her mother and her father's girlfriend. Her mother encouraged abortion. She feared adoption would leave too many scars. Nine months of pregnancy while still in school would be physically exhausting and emotionally trying for Denise. And once the child was actually born, would Denise be able to part with it? Her mother feared she would not. And if she did, she might spend her entire life wondering how her child was doing.

Denise's parents were divorced, and her father's girlfriend strongly opposed abortion. The woman tried everything to change Denise's mind. Finally, she said: "Do you know what you're doing, Denise? You might as well take a gun and take a baby and blow it away. It's the same thing."

Denise felt anxious trying to make the right choice, to make the decision that would be best for her. In the end, she chose abortion. But she knew her decision—no matter what she chose—would cause much turmoil in the family.

Because such situations often bring turmoil, some girls refuse to face the reality of their pregnancy. They secretly hope if they do not do any-

Teenagers faced with pregnancy sometimes avoid making decisions because of the turmoil their situations may bring.

thing it might just go away.

Pregnancy, however, does not just go away. And the longer one waits, the more complicated the decisions get. Ninety percent of all abortions take place early, sometime in the first twelve weeks when the fetus is still so tiny the procedure can be done safely. These abortions can be performed in a single day. Those that occur later are more expensive and require an additional visit to the doctor. At this point, the size and development of the fetus makes an abortion much more difficult. While only 10 percent of abortions take place under these circumstances, half of all late procedures are performed on teenagers.

Many girls wait several months into the pregnancy before taking action. If a girl's periods are normally irregular, she may not even realize she is pregnant until several months have passed. And even those who experience the telltale signs of pregnancy—nausea, sore breasts, and fatigue—may not admit the truth to themselves. They are terrified of the consequences. The girl may have no one to turn to, or she may not know her options. Avoiding the predicament is easier than facing the facts.

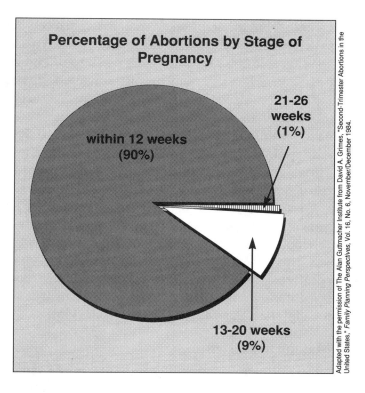

Percentage of Abortions by Stage of Pregnancy

within 12 weeks (90%)

21-26 weeks (1%)

13-20 weeks (9%)

Adapted with the permission of The Alan Guttmacher Institute from David A. Grimes, "Second-Trimester Abortions in the United States," *Family Planning Perspectives*, Vol. 16, No. 6, November/December 1984.

Carol knew her period was late and suspected she might be pregnant. She had heard people say she could expel the fetus by soaking in hot baths every night. So, she tried this on several occasions. But it turned out to be nothing more than a myth. Normal menstrual bleeding never began. Finally, with the coaxing of a friend, she called a clinic. The clinic performed a sonogram, a procedure that allows a doctor to view the fetus with a machine that uses sound waves to create a picture. Carol was twenty weeks pregnant. In another month the fetus would be more developed and an abortion would be difficult to obtain.

After approximately sixteen weeks, an abortion becomes more complicated—both medically and emotionally. The pregnancy is no longer an abstract concept, verified only by the color-coded strip of a home pregnancy test. Now, the girl feels kicking from the fetus and her stomach has begun to protrude.

Why do teenagers often wait so long to end a pregnancy? If a girl comes in for a late abortion, Ingrid Qirko of Planned Parenthood says, "It usually means that she has been denying the pregnancy all along. Or else she's been trying to decide, going back and forth in her mind. Sometimes you have some that are hoping they'll miscarry and that's why they wait."

Qirko adds that abortions are rarely easy for girls at any stage of pregnancy. "I think that very few come and go with no emotions. Physically it's uncomfortable for them. Even if they are comfortable with the decision, they're frightened. It's emotional for them, it's scary, it's embarrassing and there is a little bit of guilt," she said.

Making a decision

Sometimes, just making a choice is the most difficult part. "I have some teenagers who absolutely refuse to have an abortion," says one pregnancy counselor in a southern California clinic. "But they don't really want to keep the baby, and don't want to give it up for adoption—and they're just so stressed out about the whole thing and their parents are pushing them one way and their boyfriend is pushing them another way."

When Morgan found out she was pregnant at age fifteen, she decided to take the situation into her own hands and not tell her parents because she suspected they would oppose an abortion. She scheduled an appointment for the procedure on her own.

Her mother, however, found some information from the clinic in Morgan's room and confronted her before the abortion took place. Morgan's parents were vehemently opposed to abortion and pressured Morgan to cancel the appointment.

Conflicting views held by family and friends sometimes complicate a pregnant teenager's effort to make a decision.

Many parents want to help their children through difficult times.

Giving in to her parents' wishes, Morgan's choices had now been whittled down to two. She could either raise the child herself—though her parents said they could not afford to help—or give up the baby for adoption. Eventually, Morgan settled on adoption, an unpopular choice among teenagers these days.

A changing culture

This was not always the case. In the 1950s, adoption was a much more popular option. Experts estimate that approximately 80 percent of babies born to teenage mothers during that decade were given up for adoption. Today, the figure has dropped to 4 percent. Why such a dramatic change? The availability of abortions may be one factor. Changing attitudes toward single parenting is another.

Melissa Dodson from the Children's Home Society, a statewide California adoption agency, explains that single parenting has become more accepted in the last few decades. "If a teen got pregnant in the early sixties," she says, "they just disappeared." A girl would visit a cousin in Kansas for some unexplained reason, for example. Nine months later, the girl would return and no one would dare ask a question.

If a girl wanted to keep her child, then she felt enormous pressure from society to marry the father. Janice gave up her baby for adoption in 1968. Though she was devastated when she had to part with the newborn, she says, "In those days, you weren't a nice girl if you were unmarried with a child."

New adoption options

Times have changed considerably since the 1950s when "good" girls did not become pregnant. Single mothers no longer carry that stigma. By the late sixties, adoption figures had dropped dramatically. In 1973, adoption became even less popular as abortion became legal and girls began choosing that option.

With the decrease in the number of babies being given up for adoption, adoption agencies have

Because abortion and single parenting are losing their stigma, adoption has lost much of its appeal among pregnant teenagers. But new adoption approaches have won over some pregnant teenagers.

had to reevaluate their policies. They have had to ask tough questions about the traditional closed-door approach to adoption, which bars access to adoption records. In the hopes of making the process easier for birth parents and adoptive parents, more open arrangements have begun to take place. More and more mothers are maintaining contact with their babies rather than having them ushered out of the delivery room at birth without ever glimpsing the child's face.

When Kaitlin got pregnant as a teenager in the late sixties, both abortion and keeping the baby were out of the question. In those days, she says, "If you loved your child, you would surrender your child to adoption."

She did not realize how desperate she would feel giving her daughter, Angela, away. Remembering the words offered to her at the time, Kaitlin says, "They told me I would forget; they told me I would go on and have a new life. They told me I would marry and have other children of my own who would replace Angela. No one told me about the lifelong trauma I would have."

Kaitlin, like so many other girls, never saw her baby, never knew the adoptive parents, never knew anything about Angela. Her depression, adoption counselors now suggest, could have been lessened if she had not been separated so abruptly and permanently from her daughter.

Open adoption

Jeanne Lindsay, author of several books on options for pregnant teenagers, says, "For many young women, open adoption takes away some of the pain. Knowing where her baby is, knowing who the parents are, and something about their child-rearing practices helps her get on with her life."

Today, many adoptions occur with varying degrees of openness. The birth mother can choose the parents-to-be from a book of descriptions. If she desires, she can meet the couple and even visit the baby after birth.

Nancy had already progressed six months into her pregnancy before she realized a baby was growing inside of her. With only three months remaining, the chance for an abortion had passed her by. At fifteen, however, Nancy knew she was too young for motherhood.

The adoption agency in her Oregon hometown offered her a long list of couples wanting to adopt a child. The first one caught her eye. Like herself, the couple was Jewish. In addition, they had always been very community-minded. Everything about them reminded her of her own family.

When Nancy met with Jerry and Rose, she felt confident about her choice. She wanted them to raise her baby. Rose had been trying to get pregnant for six years without success. Jerry, Rose, and Nancy continued to meet throughout the pregnancy. When the baby was born, the adoptive parents stood by. During the first year, Nancy made regular visits to the family.

While open adoption allows the birth mother to maintain ties with her child, Dodson stresses, it does not mean shared parenting. "You're giving up all rights to parent that child. But you're not giving up your rights to love that child or to care about them for the rest of your life."

Listening to friends

In spite of the new choices available through open adoption, many girls disregard the possibility before hearing the whole story. Many do not realize how adoption has changed over the years. In other cases, they have heard tales of mothers who relinquished babies decades ago, mothers who never held or saw their children.

Most teenagers care deeply about what their friends think, and this sometimes influences their decisions.

Other teenagers, however, are fully informed and still decide against adoption. Giving a child away is not easy for anyone. As Jeanne Lindsay says, "A fifteen-year-old mother has those same feelings of intense love for her child even before it is born."

Aside from dealing with her own feelings toward the baby, a young girl feels the influence of her friends. "There is a tremendous amount of peer pressure for kids in all aspects of their lives," Dodson says. "I think when they find themselves pregnant, there's usually a tremendous amount of pressure on them to keep the baby."

Carrie wrestled with the adoption decision. She was concerned about what others would think if she gave up her baby. "People in our class at school would talk about another girl who was giving up her baby. They said, 'How can she do that after going through all that pain?' I told some of them it takes more love to give a baby up than it does to keep it!"

Carrie's words can be all too true. Giving a child up rarely comes easily. Those who do it make that choice because they understand their

Prospective teenage parents are often not aware of how much patience and maturity are required to rear a child.

own limitations. They know their child needs more love and support than they can offer.

Many teenagers have never faced such an important decision before. They do not know how to plan realistically for the future. Some say no to adoption without first answering some of the hard questions. Will they have the money for diapers, clothes, day care, food, and the many additional expenses? Will they have the patience to deal with a fussy baby, a temperamental toddler, and ultimately a rebellious teenager? Will they have the time to finish school, develop a career, and still be available as a mother?

At Life House in La Mesa, California, a home for pregnant teenagers, girls learn about the adoption option and try to sort through these issues before the birth. In six years, thirty-five girls have lived in the house. Of those, four have given their babies to adoptive parents. The others are rearing their children themselves. Unfortunately, director Caroline Fryer says, many do not realize ahead of time how difficult that path will be. "I've had too many girls come back to me," Caroline remarks, "and say, 'I wish I had looked at adoption.'"

Taking the adoption path

Why do some girls finally decide to give their babies up for adoption? Those who choose adoption tend to be "extremely determined and self-confident," one 1984 survey found. These are girls who have hopes and plans for the future. A baby, they realize, may prevent them from achieving their goals.

Aside from their own plans, these girls keep the baby's future in mind, also. As teenagers without skills or income, they realize they do not have the resources to give the child what it needs.

Anna experienced much turmoil when she gave up her daughter. She tried to take her baby back but finally decided that adoption would be best for the child. Reflecting on her situation, she offers advice to other pregnant girls: "Teens need to separate their emotions from their intelligence. So many girls keep their babies and say, 'I'll do the best I can.' I could have said that, but I know darn well that would not be the best for my daughter. I could buy her food and clothes, I could work. But what if she became terribly sick, how would I pay for the hospital?"

Even if a girl decides on adoption, she may not always have the support of her family or the baby's father. Maria faced enormous pressure from her mother and grandmother. "My grandma," she says, "couldn't handle the fact that I was giving up the child. She would cry on the phone and tell me it was almost killing her. My mother would tell me all sorts of terrible things about adoption."

Fortunately for Maria, the story had a happy ending. After the baby was born, she and her grandmother stayed in touch with the adoptive parents. They sent care packages to the baby and talked frequently to the new parents. In the end, her grandmother understood Maria's point of view and told her she had made a wonderful choice.

No single solution

Every teenager makes a different choice, and that decision will affect the rest of his or her life. Some are influenced by parents, others by friends. And some find the answers on their own. But no one knows if today's decisions will be right for tomorrow. As Jeanne Lindsay says, "First of all, we must accept the reality that there may be no one great solution for everybody." And then we must accept the fact that for some, perhaps many, no path will be an easy one.

4

A Child for Keeps

ABORTION OR ADOPTION is not the answer for every teenager. Many choose to give birth and raise their children. In the past, most girls got married before having a baby. Today, more and more teenage mothers raise their children alone, without marrying the father.

Society's attitude toward single parents has shifted dramatically during these times. Four decades ago, six out of seven pregnant girls married the father of the child. By the late 1980s, those numbers had dropped significantly. Today, single parenting has become more accepted, and consequently, teenage marriage rates have gone down. Only one-third of the teenage couples expecting a baby chose marriage. And even those who do choose marriage have little reassurance that the union will last. Within five years, at least 60 percent of married teenagers divorce.

Kim realized that at age fifteen, her chances of a lasting marriage were slim. But her boyfriend, Josh, hoped they could make it work. When Kim told him about her pregnancy, Josh thought they could settle down and have a perfect storybook family. Kim, however, knew the relationship had been a mistake from the beginning. The two eventually went their separate ways, and Kim raised the baby on her own.

(Opposite page) With the growing acceptance of single parenting, many teenagers choose to give birth and rear their children—often alone.

45

Joel Pett/*Lexington Herald-Leader.* Reprinted with permission.

Single parenting, as an alternative to marriage, can take different forms. Some girls live at home with their families, while others try to make it on their own, either with the help of the baby's father or by themselves.

Regardless of how a teenager chooses to raise her child, she will encounter similar challenges and frustrations. At any age, parenthood can be exhausting and overwhelming. Teenagers, single or married, have an added burden. Teenage mothers and fathers normally have not finished school, and obtaining a diploma once the baby arrives presents many difficulties. Without completing high school, however, adolescents are rarely prepared to support themselves, much less their children.

The Center for Population Options, an organization dedicated to preventing teenage pregnancy, states that young mothers are less likely to finish high school than their friends without children. In fact, one-fourth of unmarried teenage mothers drop out of school, and three-fourths of married teenage mothers never receive a diploma. Teenage fathers are also less likely to finish high school. One study showed that only 39 percent of teen fathers received their diploma by age twenty, as opposed to 86 percent of male teenagers who did not become fathers. In addition, teenage mothers make less money over their lifetime than those who put off having children until their twenties.

Trying to stay in school

Experts argue about the role of pregnancy and early parenting in leading teenagers down the path of poverty, off the career track, and directly into the welfare system. The relationship among these events is not clear-cut.

What is known, though, is that parenting requires enormous time and energy. Completing school with a child can be complicated and frustrating. Unlike most adolescents who have only themselves to worry about, teenage parents carry extra responsibilities. Their own needs no longer come first. Even a dedicated student might fall

Keeping up with the demands of school can be difficult for a teenage parent.

Some teenage parents do finish high school. This young mother has the advantage of attending a high school with a program for young parents.

behind in his or her schoolwork because a baby demands so much time and attention. Quiet moments for studying become rare and unpredictable. And without a high school diploma, young adults find themselves unqualified for most job positions. In spite of the pressures, not all teenage parents are doomed to failure. Many do complete high school and achieve success, but only after overcoming substantial odds.

Charlene gave birth to her daughter at sixteen and ultimately graduated at the top of her class. She struggled to achieve her goal every step of the way. Each day, she would rise early enough to dress herself and her daughter, Melanie, eat a quick breakfast while feeding Melanie, then drop her little girl at the day-care center and make it to school for an 8:00 A.M. class. "Just getting Melanie up and dressed seemed like a full day to me," Charlene says, remembering her exhaustion.

In the evenings, Charlene held Melanie on her lap as she studied. "I just gave her a pencil and some paper and we studied together." Charlene added, "Being a teenage mother is not easy at all. If some girl says she wants to have a baby, she just thinks she does. She should find a little cousin she can spend time with."

Without skills or a high school diploma, teenage parents often end up in minimum-wage positions or on welfare. In either case, they barely earn enough to support themselves and their children. Those who complete high school have more career opportunities. In the end, by obtaining a secure and well-paying job, they can take better care of their families.

Child care

By staying in school, however, teenage parents must juggle many responsibilities: finding a reliable, affordable baby-sitter, attending school, and keeping up with homework. Some teenage parents are lucky to have family assistance. But if family members cannot help take care of the baby, teenagers must turn to baby-sitters. Costs run high, and parents must carefully screen individuals and day-care centers to make sure that their child is properly cared for.

More than three hundred schools around the country are trying to help their teenage students deal with the day-care dilemma. These schools provide centers right on-site. Teenage parents can bring their children with them to school. At least 800,000 teenage parents, however, need child care. Only a small fraction benefits from school-based programs.

In the end, many teenage parents rely on a mix of both baby-sitters and family help. Sometimes, this works out. Kristine graduated from high

On-campus day care at some schools allows teenage parents to bring their children to school and attend classes. But few schools provide this service.

school, and her community college did not offer any day-care facilities. At nineteen, she lived in a small apartment complex with her mother, Nina, and baby, Megan, in California. Once she saved enough money, she planned to get an apartment with her boyfriend, Carl. It would be some time, however, before she could afford to move. For the moment, her welfare check went for baby-sitter expenses during school and work hours.

Carl watched the baby on weekends sometimes. And periodically, Kristine even went out in the evenings if she was not too tired. Her mother was willing to stay home with her grandchild. But before she went out, Kristine had to make sure that Megan was fed, bathed, and settled quietly into bed. Kristine's mother made it clear that Megan was Kristine's responsibility. Nina was not interested in starting motherhood all over again.

Others may depend completely on family members for baby-sitting. But sometimes, a supportive and helpful family is not enough. Nicole's father watched her daughter, Elizabeth, when Nicole was trying to complete her studies. Even with her father's assistance, Nicole found it difficult to finish school. She eventually dropped out because it was so hard to leave her daughter behind each day. When the baby was sick or crying, Nicole had a terrible time pulling herself away. She seemed to be constantly running out the door late for school. Once in class, she was unable to concentrate and failed two subjects.

Isolation from friends

Once the baby has been attended to and the homework done, there is rarely time for fun with friends. Young parents often feel isolated from their old friends because spending time together becomes so complicated.

Sheronda said her friends could not understand

how different her life was after the baby was born. They did not realize that she was now looking after two people instead of one. From the second she woke up in the morning, Sheronda had to keep the baby in mind. The child first needed her diapers changed, then needed to be fed, and then dressed. Only then could Sheronda consider her own needs. She would take a shower if time permitted and if the baby was not too fussy in her rocker outside the shower door. Then, Sheronda would dress herself and eat breakfast on her way out. After school, the baby needed still more attention: more diaper changes and more feedings. Sheronda's friends continued inviting her to the mall and out dancing as they always had. They did not understand why she could not just leave the baby and go.

A hungry baby will not wait. After the baby is fed there is often little time for going out with friends.

At first, Sheronda tried to keep up, tried to maintain the life-style of a tenth-grade teenager. But finally, she realized she could not do it anymore. As a parent, she could not just grab her sweater and go as she once had. "You need to take so much stuff every time you go anywhere," she comments. "You have to have a bottle, a pacifier, the stroller, extra clothes and diapers too. It just became too much of a hassle."

Now, she mostly stays home. Her friends without children do not understand how such a cute baby can also be such a burden.

The financial reality

Because they have little or no experience living on their own, many teenagers have no idea how much it costs to rear a child.

"I never realized how much it would cost to have a baby," sixteen-year-old Jeanette said. "You need to buy Pampers and formula and all kinds of things." Still in high school, she does not have time to hold down a job. At sixteen, how does

This nineteen-year-old mother of two (seated) lives with her mother. Because of the cost of rearing children, this is a common arrangement.

Jeanette make it?

For now, the government helps Jeanette with a welfare check for a few hundred dollars each month from a program called Aid to Families with Dependent Children (AFDC). She lives with her parents, so she does not have to worry about fully supporting herself. But Jeanette still contributes one hundred dollars each month from her AFDC money to help with rent. With the remaining funds, she needs to buy diapers, formula, clothes, and food for her son, Jeremy, who is twenty months old. As he gets older, her expenses will continue to grow. Jeremy will probably have his eye on a fancy bike or an expensive play car. He will want to go out for hamburgers with his friends and buy ice-cream cones.

Jeanette hopes to stick with her studies and eventually get off welfare. She is dreaming about nursing school and one day supporting her small family.

Government aid

Jeanette is not alone in her struggles. Many teenage mothers receive government aid. As high school students, they do not have the time or skills to maintain a job. According to the Alan Guttmacher Institute, 54 percent of twenty-four-year-old women who had their first baby before they were eighteen live in poverty.

The cost to the country of supporting so many young mothers is enormous. In 1988, the United States spent $19.83 billion for payments to families started when the mother was a teenager. The money went to AFDC, Medicaid, and the agency that administers food stamps. These programs assist parents with food, medicine, and other bills.

The figures were tabulated by the Center for Population Options, which estimates that almost half of that money could have been saved if these teenagers had delayed parenthood until their twenties, until they had developed job skills and were able to support their children.

Parenting

Teenage parents, however, need more than economic security. In order to provide the child with a good home, teenage mothers and fathers must develop parenting skills. Many think the task comes naturally. But parenting, like any other occupation, requires understanding, practice, knowledge, and much patience. These qualities often come with greater life experience. In addition, new parents need models. They need examples to follow. If a teenager's own parents were caring and attentive, then he or she will most likely be a loving parent. Teenagers who grow up in uncertain households, filled with violence and abuse, however, tend to mistreat their own chil-

Many pregnant young women depend on government assistance, including government-funded health clinics.

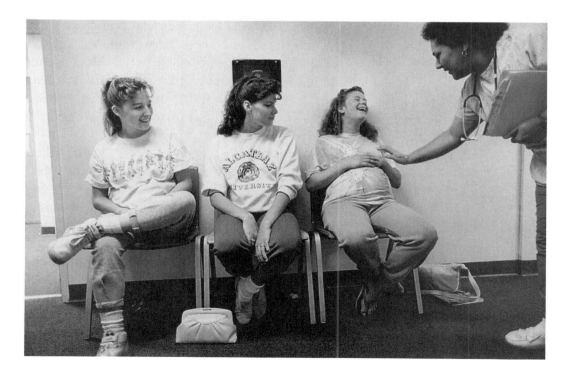

dren in the same way.

Unfortunately, many teenagers who have children grew up in less than ideal homes. Sharon Weremiuk, who works in a program for teenage parents in San Diego, estimates that 80 percent of the girls she sees come from unstable homes. In some cases, the parents fought and yelled incessantly. In others, the girls were beaten or sexually abused. These girls do not know how to be good parents because they have never seen how a "good" parent acts.

Neglect

In one extreme situation, Natalie, a twenty-three-year-old mother from a poor urban neighborhood on the East Coast, left her two children at home overnight while she went out partying. Her oldest daughter, Clarissa, was six; the baby was just nine months old. In the morning, Natalie called to ask Clarissa if she had prepared the bottles. Clarissa was terrified. She could not even reach the cupboard where the formula was kept.

Natalie did not know any better. Her mother had also been a teenage parent. Natalie, too, had been left alone when her mother went out on dates. Natalie was simply doing as her own mother had done.

Of course, not all teenage parents neglect their children. Nonetheless, some may do things they later regret, not because they are bad people but because they never learned the skills of parenting. These young adults are not prepared to deal with the confusing behavior of an infant or toddler. One moment, the baby is cute and delightful. The next minute, the baby screams and whines, rips up treasured books, and colors with crayons on prized possessions.

New parents feel frustrated by their children. They will scold frequently and wonder why the

Parenting can be exhausting at any age.

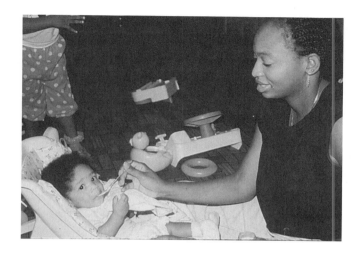

Teenagers sometimes lack the life experience and maturity that help older parents cope with a growing child's daily needs.

child does not listen. Often, parents do not realize that babies are *supposed* to do these things. Babies are curious. They like to explore and learn, and their ways are very different from the ways of older people.

All parents, young and old, can become terribly upset with tiny, helpless babies. Young parents, however, sometimes feel more impatient. They themselves may feel helpless and unable to deal with their children. Under this kind of pressure, some parents hit or slap their children to make them behave.

"Before Jeffrey was two, I hit him too hard a couple of times. But I'm coping all right now," says eighteen-year-old Jennifer. "Girls my age are more likely to abuse because when you're alone and you have to fend for yourself, it's harder."

Teenage fathers

Girls get pregnant, have babies, and become teenage mothers. But they do not fall into this predicament alone. What role do the teenage fathers play?

Some fathers help care for their children, hold down jobs, and support the new family. They

Some teenage mothers look to parenting support groups for help. Sometimes these programs neglect the needs of teenage fathers.

push themselves to the limit to give their kids a good life. There are others, however, who never see their children, who leave town as soon as they find out a baby is due.

According to a 1989 article published by the Alan Guttmacher Institute, only 16 percent of those fathers of children born to teenage mothers lived with their children. Of the absent fathers, only one-third were still visiting the child at least once a week after his or her first birthday.

Why do so many boys ignore the responsibilities of fatherhood? Many come from homes where their own father was absent while they were growing up. Others were brought up by parents who, like themselves, were teenagers who lacked parenting skills. Good role models were missing. Although boys frequently do not take part in caring for their babies, that does not necessarily mean they are not interested.

A 1985 Ford Foundation study found that teenage fathers were more than willing to participate, but they were not sure how to go about it or what to do. Most parenting programs are geared to helping the mothers, sometimes neglecting the fathers. The study found that when boys are included, they are eager to take part. In fact, once these boys did participate, their grades improved, they found work, and spent more time with their kids. In addition, the new fathers found they were not alone in facing the overwhelming task of parenting.

Taking part

James participated in a program directly aimed at young fathers. At nineteen, he thought he was not interested in sharing his feelings with a bunch of strangers. But his girlfriend, Janice, coaxed him into attending this group for teenage fathers that met in San Francisco. James surprised himself. "It changed my mind completely. I thought I was alone, that I was the only one in the world who was going to be a teen father. I didn't know

Few teenage fathers take part in rearing their children. Those who do find the experience both difficult and rewarding.

what I was going to do, basically I didn't. And I found out that I was wrong. I'm not alone," he said.

Teenagers have a hard enough time learning to be good fathers, James adds, but society makes it even more difficult. The boy is blamed for getting the mother pregnant, he explains. In addition, he says, most adults assume the father will not stick around to care for the child.

While some teenage fathers do ignore their role and abandon the situation entirely, many others wish to participate. Unfortunately, they are often caught in a bind. They can drop out of school and work to bring in some money for immediate needs, like diapers and formula, or continue studying, with future career goals in mind.

In the long run, without a high school diploma, job options will be limited. A minimum-wage job

Like teenage mothers, teenage fathers have a tough time staying in school and supporting their children.

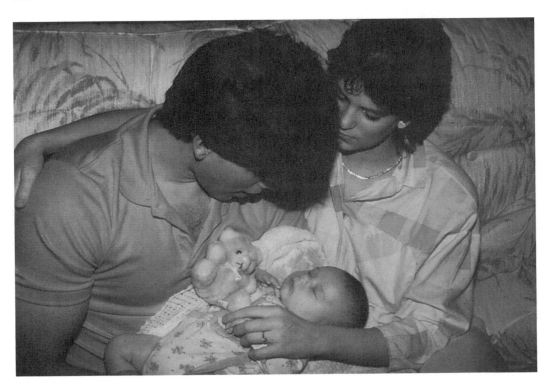

at a fast-food restaurant will not cover all of the family's expenses. Many parenting programs realize that helping young people stay in school can be as important as teaching them to change a diaper. Their key to future success lies with the high school diploma.

No easy answers

Becoming a parent can be overwhelming at any age. Young girls and boys, however, have the odds stacked against them. Without job or parenting skills and less than two decades of life experience, young mothers and fathers face many disadvantages.

How can early parenting be prevented in the first place? Many believe sex education and access to birth control are the answer. Others argue that these are the source of the problem, that these give teenagers the desire to engage in sexual activity. And still others are unsure which is the best approach. Society has struggled for generations over these issues.

Many parenting programs urge teenage parents to stay in school. Sometimes teachers in these programs take an active role in helping students care for their children.

5

Human Sexuality: To Teach or Not to Teach

TEENAGE PREGNANCY OCCURS for several reasons. Many believe ignorance about sexuality plays a major role. If that is true, who should teach young people the facts and what should they learn?

At one extreme are those opposed to any form of instruction or discussion related to sex that occurs outside the home. At the other end are those who rally for extensive education in the schools along with convenient health services providing contraceptives. The majority of people, however, probably fall somewhere in between. They want their children to be informed but have mixed feelings about the best approach.

Continuing debate

Confusion about sex education is apparent in society's policies. From sex education to school-based clinics, adults in the United States have failed to reach any consensus. They continue to search for the best method of informing teenagers about sexuality.

For several decades, sex education has been dis-

(Opposite page) Teenagers find themselves in the middle of an ongoing debate over who should tell them about human sexuality, when this should be done, and what information should be passed on.

cussed and debated, banned in some schools, and required in others. Some parents who feel uncomfortable with the subject or who are themselves poorly informed find it easier to let the schools do the job. Others may be uneasy but prefer to assume the responsibility themselves. These parents want assurance their kids will learn about sex from the family's moral perspective. Other parents are not sure how or when to discuss sexuality with their children. How much are teenagers ready to hear, they ask themselves? If they explain too much, will the children misinterpret their actions and assume the parents approve of early sexual activity? If they do not teach enough, will their children rely on rumors rather than facts? Advocates of sex education believe it is better to be fully informed than to be misinformed or ignorant.

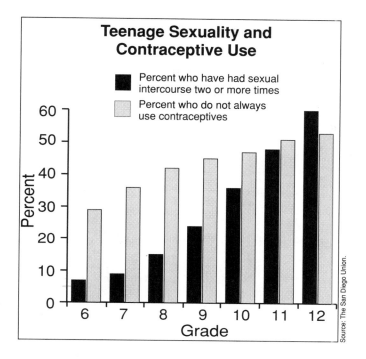

Teenage Sexuality and Contraceptive Use

■ Percent who have had sexual intercourse two or more times

▨ Percent who do not always use contraceptives

Source: The San Diego Union.

"Our failure to tell children what they want and need to know is one reason we have the highest rates of teen pregnancy and abortion in any highly developed country in the world," says sex education expert Sol Gordon.

Parents are concerned, however, about conveying their values along with the necessary facts. Many prefer that their children avoid sex until they are older and married. Some with extreme views disapprove entirely of the manner in which schools teach sexuality. In some cases, when classes in sex education are offered, these parents keep their children home from school. They believe learning about sex is the first step toward engaging in sexual activity.

"If I explain the various forms of birth control to my child, that means I approve of sex before marriage," says Kathy, a seventeen-year-old, single mother-to-be who believes that pregnancy is the price she has to pay for making the mistake of

Some schools teach students the basics of sex and childbirth. Some also explore other aspects of human sexuality. Other schools leave sex education to parents.

having sex too young. "I think premarital sex is wrong," she adds.

Sex education, however, includes more than simple lessons on birth control. Courses vary tremendously. Some schools aim to educate students about the specific facts of sex—how babies are made and how to prevent pregnancy with contraception. Others have a wider, more comprehensive goal. The classes focus on general concepts, ideas that help students shape their values and learn about the responsibilities of being an adult. Courses cover topics such as family finances, parenting roles, and communication skills.

"Sex educators now spend as much time helping students determine what they want to do with their lives and how to achieve their goals as they do on the biological aspects of reproduction," says Sylvia Schechter, director of health and physical education for the New York City school system.

Aside from discussing values, a few specialized courses focus specifically on teaching students to postpone sex until marriage. Instructors do not discuss birth control options. Instead, they stress the benefits of abstinence. They try to help adolescents feel comfortable saying "no" to early sexual relations. Many groups that oppose sex education in general support these courses.

Many educators also recommend that teenagers abstain from sex. But should these students learn about other options? Authors of abstinence-based programs believe to do so only invites trouble. They claim that teenagers will take it as a sign that having sex is okay.

While many educators agree that abstinence is the best contraceptive, they see drawbacks in programs that do not teach students about other forms of birth control. These teachers believe that young people will have sex no matter what parents or other adults say. If that is the case, they argue, the teenagers should know about contraception so they can avoid unwanted pregnancy.

"If it were up to me," says Alex Weir of the San Diego Adolescent Pregnancy and Parenting Program, "I would say wait until you're married. But let's be realistic: young people are going to have sex just like adults are going to go to sleep. You can't tell them what to do. However, if that's what they're going to choose and they will [choose sex], tell them: please do it safely, please be prepared to pay the price."

School-based clinics

If teenagers are going to have sex, regardless of advice from others, as people like Weir believe, the next logical step may be to see that they do it safely and avoid unwanted pregnancy. As a result, some schools have created on-campus clinics that offer a range of birth control-related services. Since 1970, more than 150 clinics have opened on junior high and high school campuses across the country. None of the clinics, however, has opened without causing some sort of debate in the community. Some of the proposed clinics, in fact, have never opened because of strong op-

position. What are the objections? Some people think it is inappropriate to provide birth control on the campus, where teenagers can easily purchase birth control without parents ever knowing. Parents fear losing control over their children's actions. Because of such concerns, some clinics provide general health services for students but do not give out contraceptives and contraceptive information. Others, such as the DuSable-Bogan Clinic in Chicago, offer contraceptive information and birth control.

When the staff members at the clinic first opened their doors at DuSable High School, however, the Pro-Life Action League was there to greet them. The league staged a two-hour protest opposing the clinic's presence. Any clinic prescribing contraceptives to teenagers does not belong on a school campus, the league stated.

The DuSable-Bogan Clinic provides a wide range of health services, including birth control information and prescriptions. During its first year of operation, 1,600 students visited the clinic, 50 pregnancies were confirmed, 150 cases of sexually transmitted diseases were diagnosed, and 291 contraceptives were prescribed.

When the clinic opened, 291 teenagers suddenly had access to contraceptives. These were teenagers who may not have sought protection otherwise. Is that good news or bad? Some say many girls at DuSable would probably be pregnant today if it were not for the clinic. Others counter that the teenagers would have abstained had the contraceptives been out of reach.

Questions of access

The arguments over school-based clinics closely resemble the heated debates surrounding sex education. Proponents explain that students who are already sexually active should have easy access to birth control. As Janet, a high school

School-based clinics, especially those that offer birth control, are hotly debated. High school students in Brooklyn, New York, show off condoms distributed at school.

student who counsels others on teenage pregnancy, comments, "A lot of the girls are embarrassed to go to the doctor; some simply don't realize they can get pregnant the first time, and others don't have anyone to talk to about sex." With birth control available at school, Janet believes, teenagers will be more likely to use it.

Will more girls engage in sex because birth control is now available, or will those who were not protected before the clinics arrived now begin taking precautions? Free-lance writer Mary Ann Kuharski believes the former is true. She thinks that when contraceptives are easily available, more teenagers are tempted to become sexually active. "There should . . . be no denying that all the efforts at 'education,' walk-in teen clinics, counseling . . . contraceptives and abortion availability, have only increased the number of young who now admit to be experimenting with sex," Kuharski says. From her point of view, school-based clinics only encourage sexual activity among teenagers.

Other countries

Given the range of opinions about teenage sexuality, Americans have developed a mixed bag of policies. Easy access to birth control is provided in some regions, while courses stressing abstinence is all that is taught to students in other parts of the country.

Some countries, however, have had an easier time establishing a national plan. By focusing on a single priority—pregnancy prevention—they have successfully introduced effective policies. In these countries, encouraging sexual abstinence is less important than this primary goal.

For example, in France, Great Britain, and Canada, the teenage pregnancy rate is half of that in the United States. Sweden's rate is one-third as high, and in the Netherlands, only one-tenth as many teens become pregnant.

What is their secret? The answer is unclear. But some point to the different attitudes toward birth control. In all these countries, girls receive birth control pills easily at clinics or from family doctors. Sixteen-year-old Samara, for example, lives in the Netherlands. For the last two years, she has been taking birth control pills prescribed by her family physician. All discussions with her doctor are confidential. "I don't ask if she has told her parents," her physician remarks. He believes that is her decision.

In general, the Dutch people believe that sexual activity among teenagers cannot be eliminated. Instead, they hope to prevent the trauma of unwanted pregnancies by making birth control easy to obtain.

If the United States adopted the same policy, would fewer girls become pregnant? No one knows for sure. Certainly other issues aside from the availability of birth control play a role. The level of poverty, for example, is higher in the United States than in the Netherlands, and teenage pregnancy rates are highest among the poor. In addition, many girls become pregnant purposefully in order to find the love they never received at home. In such cases, these young women need more than birth control. They need a brighter future.

A multisided debate

Although the statistics from Europe seem encouraging, European policies will not necessarily work in the United States. Americans have too many different opinions to readily adopt programs aimed solely at pregnancy prevention.

This point was clearly illustrated in 1991 when Governor Pete Wilson of California proposed that

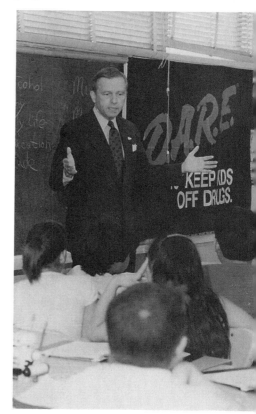

California governor Pete Wilson stirred up controversy when he proposed that Norplant be offered to teenagers and drug addicts to reduce unwanted pregnancies.

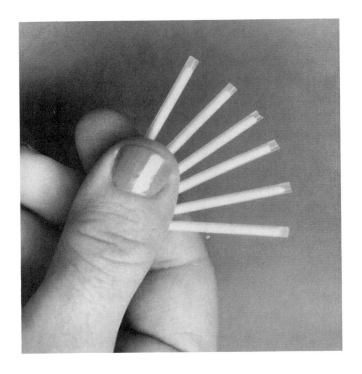

Norplant birth control capsules are inserted under the skin of a woman's upper arm and are effective for five years.

teenagers and drug addicts be given easy access to a new form of birth control called Norplant. The new contraceptive offers a distinct advantage over the traditional birth control pills, which must be taken daily. Once Norplant is inserted just beneath the skin under the arm, it lasts for five years. A girl can ignore it completely and still be safe from pregnancy.

Wilson's proposal prompted swift and varied response from California residents. Two letters to the editor of the *Los Angeles Times* illustrate the range of opinions on the subject. One letter writer applauded Wilson's proposal: "Wilson's plan to make Norplant contraception available to teenagers and drug users is one of the most far-sighted, intelligent proposals made by a political leader in a long time. It will do a lot to reduce welfare dependency, school dropouts and crime by the unwanted and neglected. The anti-contraception forces must not be allowed to defeat this proposal."

Another letter writer criticized the plan: "Wilson's proposal to make Norplant widely available to teenagers is mind-boggling. In essence, the message given to our young is that they can participate in promiscuous sexual activity and never bear any of the consequences, i.e. pregnancy."

With such strong and different opinions, it is easy to see why the United States has not adopted a unified approach to curbing teen pregnancy. The population of the country is unable to agree on a single goal. That does not mean, however, that no efforts are being made to fight the problem. Concerned citizens throughout the country have developed programs for teenagers that represent a range of cultural, religious, and political perspectives.

6

Breaking the Cycle

EACH YEAR, ONE MILLION American girls get pregnant. Approximately half of them deliver babies. The others have abortions. While many teenagers do become good parents, develop careers, and support themselves, many others are forced to rely on welfare and have even more babies. Their children grow up and repeat the same patterns, becoming young parents themselves.

Can the cycle be broken? Can these parents ever offer their children a better way of life? In different regions of the United States, concerned individuals are devoted to breaking the cycle by helping teenagers who have had babies and by helping those who are at risk of becoming young parents. Each group has a different approach. Each is trying to tackle the complex issue from a different angle.

Flour-sack babies

Robert Valverde, a sex education teacher at Mission High School in San Francisco, wanted his students to get a taste of the real world of parenting. He wanted them to experience parenting firsthand but without actually having a baby. He wanted his students to know what it is like to

(Opposite page) Concerned individuals and groups throughout the United States are committed to reducing the staggering number of teenage pregnancies and keeping teenagers in school.

73

Many teenagers cannot imagine the amount of responsibility that child-rearing requires.

have continuous responsibility for another individual. Perhaps then they would see what is truly involved in the task, before it was too late to turn back. He wanted his students to see that babies are more than little playmates and to be aware of how much work is involved in caring for a child.

Valverde surprised his students when he showed up one day in class dressed like a surgeon fresh from the operating room, complete with hospital scrubs, cap, mask, and booties. What was Valverde up to?

The students soon found out. "Welcome to the nursery," Valverde said. "Please don't breathe on the babies. I just brought them from the hospital." The "babies," which Valverde promptly delivered to each student, were actually five-pound sacks of flour. Each student received one. And each student had to take care of that flour-sack child for the next three weeks.

"You must treat your baby as if it were real twenty-four hours a day," Valverde announced. "It must be brought to every class. You cannot put the baby in your locker or your backpack. It must be carried like a baby, lovingly and carefully in your arms. Students with jobs or other activities must find baby-sitters."

During that three weeks, Valverde would call various students at home to find out how the baby was doing. If the baby was lost, they were awarded an even bigger baby—a ten-pound sack of flour.

Here to stay

At first, the students enjoyed Valverde's game. They dressed their sacks in cute little baby clothes, carried bottles and diapers, and enjoyed playing parents. By the second week, however, that five- or ten-pound sack of flour started to feel like quite a load. The students were beginning to understand the strenuous side of parenting. Having a child, they began to realize, means more than showing off a darling infant to friends. It means carrying those five or ten pounds every-

where. Once the baby is born, it is there to stay. There is no escaping the child, they learned, even when it starts to weigh the parent down.

"Why does it have to be so heavy?" complained Latoya, a student in Valverde's class. "It's raining out—how am I supposed to carry this baby and open my umbrella at the same time?" Aside from the frustrations of lugging the five-pound baby everywhere, Latoya also noticed how differently people treated her. "There is no way a boy is even going to look at me when I have this in my arms. No guys want to be involved with a girl who has a baby—they just stay clear."

At the end of three long weeks, many of the flour-sack babies had been dumped in the trash. Many of the student-parents were exhausted. "After this class," another student commented, "I don't want to have a baby. I couldn't handle it. It was only a sack of flour that didn't cry or scream, didn't need to be fed or put to sleep, and I still couldn't wait to get rid of it."

Harlem

Across the country in New York City, another teacher hopes to help students delay parenting. Michael Carrera, a professor of health sciences at Hunter College in New York, developed a program for teenagers in Harlem, one of the city's poorest neighborhoods.

With high dropout rates in the schools and few available jobs, these young adults had few options. The majority came from families where parents worked at low-paying jobs, were on welfare, or had joined the violence and terror of drug dealing. For many of these young adults, having children was their only possibility for happiness.

Carrera had a plan. He wanted to show these students that they actually had many more choices. Life was not limited to what they saw in

Michael Carrera directs a program aimed at keeping teens in school and preventing early pregnancy.

Carrera (top right) talks to a group of teenagers in West Harlem. One way to prevent teenage pregnancy, Carrera believes, is to provide teenagers with opportunities and help them develop self-esteem.

their immediate surroundings.

The first step to achieving higher goals, Carrera believed, was developing self-esteem. The teenagers had to believe in themselves. And so Carrera offered programs through the Children's Aid Society. The programs were designed to help teenagers boost their confidence.

He wanted to create a place where young adults would learn more than the basics of sexuality. Helping teens set goals would help them understand why early parenting often resulted in dead-end futures. The center would be a warm environment where kids could congregate and feel safe. Many of these young people did not receive such support in their own homes. "We must offer teens the resources and opportunities that will provide them with a sense of the future and reasons not to become pregnant," Carrera says. "It is possible to convince teens to forego early pregnancy and childbearing if they have a more hopeful sense of their future."

Carrera's program brgan in 1985. It provides opportunities for teenagers and gives them a sense of a greater purpose in their lives. Young people participate in a job club and areer awareness program. Tutors assist with homework so the students have a better chance of finishing school.

Finding help

The participants also take part in workshops where they explore issues relevant to their lives, and where they learn skills that help them cope with their problems. In addition, students participate with their parents in a fifteen-week class in family life and sex education. Any student who completes high school or passes an equivalency exam and participates fully in the program is guaranteed admission to Hunter College and is eligible for financial help.

"This program helped shape what I want to be, what to look forward to," explains Diana. Having completed Carrera's program, Diana accepted a scholarship from Hunter College, an achievement beyond her wildest dreams.

With emotional and financial support from Carrera's program, Diana was on her way to having a career. She was relieved to have survived the tumultuous years of adolescence without a baby in her arms. Diana says: "The program helped me deal with pressures, such as sexual pressures. It's hard being a teenager. There's so much pressure, it's unbelievable."

During the center's first five years of operation, twenty participants went on to college. With three hundred teenagers and their parents taking part in activities, only six girls became pregnant and only two boys fathered a child. Such numbers are in sharp contrast to the statistics in the surrounding Harlem neighborhood, where seventy girls in every hundred become pregnant before their twentieth birthday.

Teenage Ninja Mothers

Programs like Carrera's or Valverde's try to prevent teenage pregnancy. Others try to help those who already have children be the best parents possible. One program in Los Angeles works with teenage mothers who are trying to complete their education. It helps them juggle the demands of school and parenthood. Each year, at least forty thousand teenagers find that balance too difficult to achieve and drop out of school. Business Industry School in Los Angeles is trying to help reverse that trend. It offers a complete program for school-age mothers, and several girls have been

By talking with each other about their experiences as parents, teenage mothers at Business Industry School in Los Angeles learn new ways of dealing with the trials of parenthood.

able to return to school and obtain their degrees. The school offers a day-care center on campus along with a support group for the mothers. Meeting five days a week with teacher Ruth Beaglehole, these girls share common struggles as they complete high school while raising children.

The learning takes place as the students discuss their own personal situations rather than in a lecture format. This way, the mothers can express their frustrations and receive encouragement and advice from Beaglehole as well as from the other mothers. The supportive atmosphere helps them gain self-confidence. Like Carrera, Beaglehole knows that if the girls believe in themselves, they can go a long way. They will be better mothers to their children and better equipped to set goals in their lives.

Hoping to share their experiences with other high school students, the girls produced a play called *Teenage Ninja Mothers*. The play offers an insider's view of the world of teenage parenting. Clearly, these girls know firsthand about the realities of teenage parenting. The task is not as glamorous as they had been led to believe. The constant attention they received during pregnancy faded quickly once the baby was born. Instead, confusion, frustration, and many tense moments are part of day-to-day life.

Reality check

The play's first scene illustrates this point: It takes place in the morning, when the teenage mother is trying to get ready for school. The baby is whining. The mother is trying to dress herself and her baby, eat breakfast, feed the baby, gather her books and the baby's things, and make it to the bus on time. During this commotion, the teenager's mother walks in to complain about the mess in her daughter's room. The girl feels exas-

A young mother at Business Industry School strengthens the bond with her children by reading to them.

perated trying to deal with a crying baby and a nagging mother.

The young mother finally makes it out of the house and to the bus with her child. In the next scene, they are riding the bus and the baby cries over and over, "Carry me, carry me," while the mother barely manages to hold onto all her other belongings. All the people on the bus are whispering, "Isn't it terrible? She's such a young mother. Look, she can't even control her child." The play continues, depicting the many challenges faced by a teenage mother.

Without these parenting classes, many young mothers would never have received a high school diploma. More important, these girls would have raised their children alone, without the encouragement of others who face the same trying circumstances. The girls would have missed an important chance to develop faith and pride both in themselves and their children.

"I believe I watch a miracle every day," Beaglehole says about the changes she witnesses. "If it is just one mother who tells me she didn't hit her child, that's a miracle."

Some schools have developed similar programs specifically for boys. At Ocean Shores High School in San Diego, Alex Weir runs a weekly session for teenage boys that teaches essential life skills. The meetings take place at the high school, which is located in a crime-ridden, gang-filled neighborhood. Weir is trying to heighten awareness and offer students a new perspective. He is helping them make the connection between sex, pregnancy, and parenting. "It's easy to plant the seed," Weir says to his students. "But who is going to be there to cultivate it, the taxpayer or you?" Will the young men stay with their children and take responsibility for raising them, or will they leave the burden to the mother and government programs?

A glimpse of parenting

Each week, these boys get a glimpse of what parenting really means. They visit the infant nursery at a local hospital, and each one takes his turn holding a baby born addicted to drugs. They see infants connected to lifesaving machinery. These infants must struggle to take each breath because their mothers did not take care of themselves during pregnancy. Weir takes the boys to dingy apartments infested with cockroaches to see how their children might live if they do not participate in their care and upbringing. He also takes them to facilities for juvenile delinquents, offering a taste of what life will be like for those who choose drugs and gangs.

Back at school, the boys learn to cook, change diapers, and care for their babies. Being a man, Weir tries to impress upon these boys, means taking responsibility. Being a man does not mean talking big, getting your girlfriend pregnant, and then leaving town. "If you're proud about planting the seed," Weir asks, "are you going to be proud about staying there and raising it?" Weir's

Some communities offer programs for teenage fathers that teach parenting skills and provide a supportive atmosphere.

strong words do sink in. He has seen kids become convinced that they must take a vital role in their children's lives.

The parenting groups at Business Industry School and Ocean Shores work because the young adults help each other. Sometimes, teenagers themselves can be the best teachers to other young people. For that reason, *L.A. Youth*, a newspaper for teenagers that is distributed to schools and libraries every other month, ran an essay contest on the subject of teenage parenting. The paper wanted to know if its readers thought teenagers were prepared to become parents. In the following winning essay, sixteen-year-old Tina Lam of Lawndale, California, describes the challenges of parenting:

> If you think you're ready for parenthood, try getting up at three, four and five o'clock in the morning to read and reread this essay. Even though you'll lose sleep and be cranky in the morning, remember that this essay doesn't have to be changed, cuddled and fed like a real live baby. Next time you are invited to go out, tell your friends you have to retype this essay 10 times. Maybe you can put off retyping this essay until later, but you can't put off a baby until later. The baby will be the main focus of your life.
>
> oDuoy llits kniht ouy era ydaer ot eb a tnerap? sI ti tluciffid ot daer eseht secnetnes? If you found those two sentences difficult to read and went straight to this one, then what do you plan to do when your baby is even more difficult to take care of? Your patience might wear thin when the baby is screaming, day after day.
>
> The important issue if you are pregnant is not who is to blame, but rather if two people can continue to love each other and care for their baby. I think I would wait until the baby is a blessing instead of a curse.

Glossary

abortion: The termination of a pregnancy by expelling the fetus during a medical procedure.

abstinence: Voluntarily refraining from sexual intercourse.

adolescence: The period of life and development that occurs during the teenage years.

adoption: Taking the biological child of other parents and raising the child as one's own; the biological parents give up legal rights to the child.

Aid to Families with Dependent Children (AFDC) or Aid to Dependent Children (ADC): A form of welfare or financial assistance offered by the government to families.

birth control: Any product or device that is used to prevent pregnancy, including pills, condoms, intrauterine devices (IUDs), diaphragms, and other devices.

contraception: Prevention of fertilization of a human egg.

food stamps: Coupons issued by the government to families with limited income. The coupons can be used to purchase food items only.

Medicaid: Medical assistance offered by the government to those with limited income.

Norplant: A new type of birth control in which six matchstick-size tubes are inserted beneath the skin under the arm. The tubes release hormones that prevent pregnancy from occurring.

prenatal care: Medical care provided to a baby before it is born. Under the best circumstances, prenatal care should begin in the first month of pregnancy, and the mother should see the doctor at least once a month until birth.

sexually transmitted disease: Any disease that is passed from one partner to the other during sexual intercourse.

single parent: One who raises a child by himself or herself, without the other parent's involvement.

uterus: The female organ in which a baby develops and grows.

welfare: Refers to any form of financial assistance from the government.

Organizations
to Contact

The following organizations deal with the issues of teenage pregnancy. Many offer publications and brochures on the topic.

Alan Guttmacher Institute (AGI)
111 Fifth Ave.
New York, NY 10003
212-254-5827

AGI works to develop adequate family planning and sex education programs through policy analysis, public education, and research. The institute publishes the bimonthly *Family Planning Perspectives* and the quarterly *International Family Planning Perspectives*.

Center for Population Options (CPO)
1025 Vermont Ave. NW
Washington, DC 20005
202-347-5700

CPO is a nonprofit educational organization dedicated to improving the quality of life for adolescents by preventing teenage childbearing. CPO's national and international programs seek to improve adolescent decision making through life planning and other educational programs, to improve access to reproductive health care, to promote the development of school-based clinics, and to prevent the spread among adolescents of HIV and other sexually transmitted diseases.

Children's Defense Fund
122 C St. NW
Washington, DC 20001
202-628-8787

This organization is a national children's advocacy group working for the rights and protection of children. Its Adolescent Pregnancy Prevention Clearinghouse publishes six reports per year on the teenage pregnancy crisis in the United States.

National Organization on Adolescent Pregnancy and Parenting, Inc. (NOAPP)
4421-A East-West Highway
Bethesda, MD 20814
301-913-0378

NOAPP serves as a national network on adolescent pregnancy care and prevention issues. The organization publishes a newsletter called *NOAPP Network.*

National Training Center for Adolescent Sexuality and Family Life Education
350 East 88th St.
New York, NY 10128
212-876-9716

The center offers training and technical assistance to agencies interested in replicating the Children's Aid Society's successful Teen Pregnancy Prevention Program.

Planned Parenthood
810 Seventh Ave.
New York, NY 10019
212-541-7800

Planned Parenthood supports individuals making decisions about reproduction without interference from the government. The organization runs clinics throughout the United States that offer family planning services.

Project Respect
PO Box 97
Golf, IL 60029
708-729-3298

Project Respect has developed a sex education curriculum called Sex Respect for junior and senior high students. The program is designed to provide teenagers with information and to encourage sexual abstinence. According to the authors of the curriculum, "Sex Respect teaches teens that saying 'no' to premarital sex is their right, is in the best interest of society and is in the spirit of true sexual freedom."

Teens Against Pre-marital Sex (TAPS)
PO Box 19662
Cincinnati, OH 45219
513-861-TAPS

The group offers courses for teenagers interested in postponing sex until marriage. It also provides a support network that allows young people to take part in a variety of social, environmental, and cultural activities.

Suggestions for Further Reading

Barbara Fitzsimmons, "A Teen Mother . . .," *San Diego Union*, April 30, 1989.

Jeanne Lindsay, *Open Adoption: A Caring Option*. Buena Park, CA: Morning Glory Press, 1987.

Jeanne Lindsay, *Parents, Pregnant Teens and the Adoption Option*. Buena Park, CA: Morning Glory Press, 1988.

Jeanne Lindsay, *Pregnant Too Soon: Adoption Is an Option*. Buena Park, CA: Morning Glory Press, 1980.

Jeanne Lindsay, *Teen Pregnancy Challenge*. Buena Park, CA: Morning Glory Press, 1989.

Paula McGuire, *It Won't Happen to Me*. New York: Delacorte Press, 1983.

Jane Marks, "We Have a Problem," *Parents*, June 1988.

Jane Claypool Miner, *Young Parents*. New York: J. Messner, 1985.

Claudia Wallis, "Children Having Children," *Time*, December 9, 1985.

Works Consulted

Lexine Alpert, "Flour Children," *In Health*, January/February 1990.

Steve Barnes, "Crusade of Dr. Elders," *New York Times Magazine*, October 15, 1989.

David L. Bender and Bruno Leone, eds. *Teenage Sexuality: Opposing Viewpoints*. San Diego: Greenhaven Press, 1988.

Kim Walsh Childers, "Sex, Media and Your Child," *Carolina Alumni Review*, Spring 1988.

Susan Christian, "Just a Kid Herself," *Los Angeles Times*, March 13, 1991.

Leon Dash, *When Children Want Children: The Urban Crisis of Teenage Childbearing*. New York: William Morrow, 1989.

Amy Engeler, "Giving Up a Baby," *Glamour*, June 1990.

Daniel B. Frank, *Deep Blue Funk & Other Stories: Portraits of Teenage Parents*. Chicago: The Ounce of Prevention Fund, 1983.

Nancy Herndon, "Parents Who Are Boys," *The Christian Science Monitor*, May 23, 1988.

Kristi Hinchmar, "It'll Never Happen to Me," *Teen*, November 1989.

Laurence Jolidon, "Not Easy at All," *USA Weekend*, June 9-11, 1989.

Barbara Kantrowitz, "High School Homeroom," *Newsweek*, Summer/Fall 1990.

Jeanne Lindsay, *Teens Parenting: The Challenge of Babies and Toddlers*. Buena Park, CA: Morning Glory Press, 1981.

Melissa Ludtke, "Giving Teenagers a New View of Their Future," *Time*, May 1, 1989.

Cheryl McCall, "Denise's Decision," *Life*, March 1986.

Elizabeth Mehren, "Study Shatters Stereotype of the Unwed Teen Father," *Los Angeles Times*, October 2, 1985.

Janet Podell, *The Reference Shelf: Abortion*. New York: H. W. Wilson, 1990.

Michael Quintanilla, "Words of Wisdom from Realistic Teenagers," *Los Angeles Times*, June 23, 1991.

Readings on Teenage Pregnancy from Family Planning Perspectives. New York: The Alan Guttmacher Institute, 1990.

Bryan E. Robinson, *Teenage Fathers*. Lexington, MA: Lexington Books, 1988.

Ken Robison, "Holistic Solution Works in Harlem," *The Fresno* (California) *Bee*, December 10, 1989.

Eloise Salholz, "Teenagers and Abortion," *Newsweek*, January 8, 1990.

Janny Scott, "Babies Are Born to Die in the Delta," *Los Angeles Times*, September 30, 1990.

"American Agenda," Teen Pregnancy Series, ABC's "World News Tonight," June 26-29, 1989.

Index

About the Author

Judy Berlfein is a free-lance writer from Encinitas, California. She writes frequently on medicine and environmental issues for magazines and newspapers. She has also been a reporter for public radio.

Ms. Berlfein received a master's degree in physiology and pharmacology from the University of California at San Diego.

Picture Credits